"Reading Raymond Antrobus's Signs, *Music*, was an exhilarating (re)ride into the wonders and terrors of becoming a new parent. It's hard to explain how much parenting can change a person, but Antrobus succeeds: 'I broke up / with announcing my convictions and good news / on the internet I broke up with talking to myself / as if I'm not there I broke up with people-pleasing / and the trembling boundary between life and still life.' Here is a beautiful mapping of a journey of this life that becomes *this* life in all of its anaphoric radiance. Each letter in these poems is bursting at the seams."

—**Victoria Chang**,
author of *With My Back to the World*

"Oh, so *this* is why I turn to poetry—not just for naming, but for the grappling to name. As a soon-to-be (and then new) father Raymond Antrobus invites us into a reckoning with this freighted identity: 'it's a whole / madness, my old / screaming selves.'

With a voice candid and intimate, Signs, *Music* teaches us that reckoning is always a more profound event than conclusion. How can one step into new responsibility consciously and lovingly, without buckling under the gathered weight of one's own childhood, one's own gendered, racial, and societal inheritances? Besides *being* a father, how does one become a father?

Antrobus holds seriously the bright needle of the lyric, pulling his questions through the rough fabric of fatherhood, and so, provokes that fabric with hole after hole. His willingness to lay bare his anxieties and share his discoveries invites us into expanded definitions and territories of 'fatherland.' Told with frankness and a masterful wielding of image, Signs, *Music* is so tenderly rendered that I found myself gasping."

—**Shira Erlichman**,
author of *Odes to Lithium*

T0182591

"Raymond Antrobus's Signs, *Music* is unlike any poetry about becoming a father I've read. A report from two different countries—the land before birth and afterwards—the strength of this book comes from what it lets stand: half-thoughts, snatched conversations, hard memories. Caffeinated anticipation gives way to exhaustion and wonder, and a darker strain of introspection. The transition from fatherlessness to fatherhood isn't smoothed over, but the son's birth allows for a reconfiguration of relationships—with Antrobus's mother, with the city he grew up in. 'They've always been here,' he writes. 'I'm just / moving slowly enough to see them.' Here is a book of slow seeing which reaches a level of genuine intimacy."

—Will Harris,
author of *Brother Poem*

"Signs, *Music* wades devotedly through weathers of joy, grief, wonderment and terror—all of which arise as fleetingly on the page as they do in the throes of new parenthood. Vulnerable and hopeful, though never expectant of certainty or utopia, Signs, *Music* is a prayer for a world that might yet look tenderly upon young black life."

—Victoria Adukwei Bulley,
author of *Quiet*

"In this honest, witty and humane book, Antrobus brilliantly pins down the before and after of parenthood—and the uncrossable gap between the two. These poems manage to look both backwards and forwards: at who we were, who we are and who we hope to be."

—Joe Dunthorne,
author of *O Positive*

"Stunning in its concise clarity, Signs, *Music* testifies to more than the process of becoming a parent for the first time. It bravely parents author and reader alike through the undeniable parallels between childhood and personhood, father-making and nation-making, while documenting the often hidden and inextricable relationship between violence and tenderness and the brutal necessity of both in the transition from human to caregiver. 'I keep asking people about children. / *How do you keep them alive?*' In his attention to sound, space, and language, Antrobus remains innocent and present, never naive, gently pointing to what we might drop from our language if we want to be remade. This is an incredible follow-up to his previous hat trick of collections."   **—Marwa Helal**, author of *Ante body*

Signs, Music

Signs, Music

poems

Raymond Antrobus

TIN HOUSE / PORTLAND, OREGON

Poetry is music from the place we are born

Contents

It's hard to reckon with where you come from.
It's hard to disentangle the ranting,
raving brutes from the modern, 'civilized'
fathers; it's hard to figure out where to place
your allegiance.

—KATHERINE ANGEL, *DADDY ISSUES*

and may you in your innocence
sail through this to that

—LUCILLE CLIFTON, 'BLESSING THE BOATS'

Signs, Music

Look at that tree and write about it.
But Mimi, I don't know the name of that tree.
I can describe it but can't distinguish it; tall, brown, bursting
with leaves like a loaded wallet,
autumn's green and yellow receipts.
It is against my nature to notice the tree. Who am I
to rustle in the wind? Mimi, my best memory
of a tree is the one that grew at the back
of my mother's garden, it might've been a young oak
or a sweet gum. My mother came back from the market with rope
and asked my father to tie it around the thickest arm,
the knot was the seat for my sister and me
so we could swing. Mimi, we sat on that knot and launched ourselves,
held our whole face and both arms and feet against the rope
and tarzaned into the air. That branch held us all summer,
my parents months from their second separation,
my sister a year from running away from home, calling
the house, hanging up on Mum's new boyfriend.
When I finally answered, *You know none of this is your fault?*
I sat on the staircase with a rubber pad on the receiver so I could listen
through hearing aids, that one bit of her voice entered me
while I stared out the window at that tree.
See, Mimi? I don't know what I'm saying, I don't know
what I'm hearing. Me?
I'm just rustling in the wind.

i

Towards Naming

I don't think my child is going to be a good person,
says someone's mother
to an expectant father. I stare
at the stain on my suede shoes
and think *this is a first world problem.*
What was the world's first problem?
Across the street a woman is locked
outside her house. She is yelling
down the phone. Chanting men
in football shirts pass by—bankers,
politicians and builders on bicycles.
Two coffee cups on an empty café table
look on. My first problem
was either shoelaces, a drunk
father, writing my *y*'s wrong or
not finishing something on my plate.

.

No offence, says my faithful friend,
sitting by the large café window,
but why have children
when the world is ending? Outside
four men sit around a table and when a dog
passes them, they lean over and ruffle
its fur and ears, one of them skinning a roll-up.
No one asks the dog's name but smoke
from the man's cigarette wafts into the café.
Behind the glass, I hold my breath.

.

No garlic in the kitchen now that your mother is carrying you.
She can't be in the same room and breathe
if there are fumes on my breath.

·

I think of naming you Orwell,
Orwell! Dinner's ready. Orwell!
Stop spying on your mother!
I'm tired of your cynicism, young man.
That's what I'm not looking forward to.
Having to tell you (Orwell?) off.
Your moods meeting my temper.

·

What was I saying?
Last night I watched a film where vampires
had reflections. At first I thought it was a mistake,
a continuity error, but soon it made sense.
They can't unsee how they're seen
after all their years coffined in the dark. *Rumi, Blake, Selvon, Son,*
maybe our myths are finally evolving?

·

The sun is rising and there's nowhere to hide.
The narrative I have of myself insists on blood.
Today is my last Father's Day as a non-father.
This time next year I'll be a different creature,
probably writing prose for that *red-hot money*.
Sleepless and hissing behind curtains.

•

The barista puts my coffee on the table
and sings out *En-joy!* like a musical doorbell,
a note struck so straight without irony or parody,
it takes me completely out of my thinking.
I watch him hurry to the next order without
pausing for applause or acknowledgement as if
he knows the way to live—as if he knows
the grace we deserve to give ourselves.
I turn up my sound and enjoy listening
to him placing hot cups on the other tables.

•

New dads are marching
at the climate change protest.
Earth rolls her eyes.

•

Your mother wants to call you Sebastian
but that's the name of the bully that snuck
into my backpack and stole my *FIFA 98*.
It's also the name of the Jamaican steel-
pan playing crab in *The Little Mermaid*
and the saint who had his chest pierced
with arrows. I can't name you
after anything I fear happening.

•

Last winter
still in Oklahoma

I stumble shivering
through the dark

looking for the switch
that won't work

I creak open
the bathroom door

and see the water
frozen in the bowl

so I wake your pregnant mother
pack a bag of clothes and drive

slowly across the 4 AM iced roads
when we draw up

to the hotel car park no one
is on the street except a woman

in a doorway in a nightgown
waving shouting *call the police*

he's going to kill me!
a man marches up

behind her and
a police car pulls

out of nowhere
I'll kill you!

shouts the man
as his wrist is clamped

with handcuffs we can't
stay here we have to drive

to another hotel
we have to brave

the icy roads that say
I could kill you

to the car as the wheels
slide over it

now we have taken
the shape of something

that loses what it knows
in the cold *I could kill you*

say the frozen trees
breaking apart

and collapsing
beside us

•

So I sing through the walls of your mother's pregnant belly,
'Three Little Birds', what my father sang
any time he saw my face troubled—

Yuh listen to Bob, nuh? Don't worry about a thing.
In the music video for 'Is This Love'
Marley bounces around at a children's party,

the boy from the government yard in Trench Town, who
once stole a guitar from a man who
refused to pay him for his song. Everything hits

in a new way the week we find a flat
in London, knowing in a few months you will be here,
which is as hypothetical as it is real.

·

In the café a man is talking,
his voice so deep the table trembles. Your mother says
you like my voice. When I call—*Ira? Darcus? Avery?*
you stop thumbing in her womb and lie still, as if
you'd been listening for some soothing clue
about who I am or where you are.

·

On my page, a fly with one hurt wing
has landed on the word *novel*.
It is crawling towards *Prague* and *Kafkaesque*.
It launches into flight from the *t* in *terror*.

I think your death would tense
all my pressure points even more
than the time in Homerton Hospital when

I held my father's fingers and tried
to pry them open, found death
had stiffened them in place.

In my hand I have nothing, in the bush is everything
wrote Kafka. Now your mother waves me out of the trance,
offers me egg on toast.

•

Your mother was sure you'd be a girl.
There was some grief when the girl
fell away.

Boy

I'm afraid of how
the world won't trust you
before you know why.

•

In the gender-neutral restroom,
I consider the urinal.

Behind me,
the door
is pushed.

Enter
a man, mohawk
dyed purple,

a woman,
diamond studded,

a man, green
eyeliner,
black-rimmed glasses.

In the bright communal
mirror I notice
my tightness—

box-stiff shoulders,
brows creased,
rigid mouth.

I relax, let it go.
Stream it out.

I hear nothing crack
or scream,
nothing

                                                  except
                                                  release

                                              of my own
                                              prickling,

                                                  my own
                                                  flowing
                                                  fluid.

                                    •

In the street, I stop, stare at the dads
with babies strapped to their chests.

They've always been here. I'm just
moving slowly enough to see them.

Tamed Dads in the dense city. Dads
who've struggled to love themselves,

love their babies
resembling them!

                                    •

            Outside a café in New York
            I heard a toddler shout

            I'm awesome!

In London, a baby in a pram is
facing away from the mother
sat sipping her coffee glaring
down at her phone.
I lock eyes with the baby.
The baby's eyes shriek

What!

will you be any better?

.

Your father has spent years
straining over his words. It feels
indulgent now, writing
while your mother is working,
I'm wondering how you
will find language; I mean, you,
being born in Bloomsbury—
Woolf, Rossetti, Tagore
commemorated in green
spaces, parks, signs, busts.

.

My lines lean towards my father (again!)
asking where his name, Seymour, came from.
He always had the same allusion:
The more I see, the more I see. He was
a man of vague poetic-sounding sayings,
allowed himself a looseness, a non-commitment
to specificity. He should've been a poet.
I modeled parts of myself on his sensibilities—
flaws, oppressions and vanities. *It matters
what you call a thing*—son, father, still talking.

.

What!

will you be any better?

.

The day after my father
had drunk, he got up early,

put his clothes on in his
smoky single room, hobbled

the half mile to my mother's
house, football under

his arm, and roused me
from my bed to keep

his promise to play
in London Fields

that morning. I knew
about his fractured toe.

When he chose
to tap the ball

with his foot
I flinched,

felt his pain roll towards me.

.

I spent the last year avoiding poets
who announce the forms they write in.
My life calmed. Became less try-hard.

Child, I want that for you.

.

Who will I be talking to years from now?
What screens will I be losing
my thoughts to? What books
will I be pulling from the shelves?
Whose laundry
will be airing on the line?
Whose name will be blaring
through all this time?

.

Freedom, wrote Camille T. Dungy, *is measured, in part, by the freedom to choose one's own name.*

Sojourner?
Seacole?
Sharpe?

Can a name suffer
the hiss of fire and air?

·

| Nasya | a miracle |
| Atlas | to endure |

| Hades | unseen |
| Eros | desire |

| Nova | beginning |
| Acre | of the land |

| Nuri | my fire |
| Astra | starry |

| Hagar | flight |

·

I find myself staring into the distance,
my mind moving over something unsayable—
When you're birthed, don't die.

·

My mother rings to apologise
about my middle name and how many lines
it has had me pulled out of,
how many questions
aimed at me in how many accents—

Where was your passport issued?
Who gave you your middle
name? Why are you here?

I want to smell the rosemary.

I want to keep your name safe.

·

I keep asking people about children.
How do you keep them alive?

·

My sign name is the BSL letter *R* (place trigger finger on dominant hand in shape of a hook, then place finger on palm of non-dominant hand, then lift dominant hand up over head, then open all fingers out in the BSL word for light, shower, sunrays).

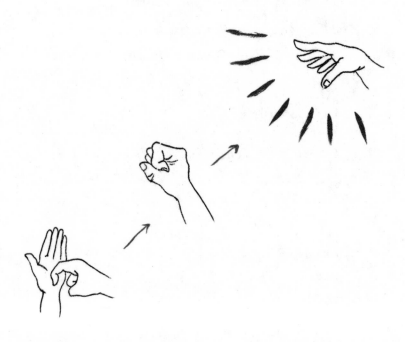

The body houses
countless feelings that can't
address their own names

When I ask my mother what I was
like as a baby, she says *the roof
needed fixing*—memory like a tile
that slips, falls slant.
You were born she repeats
*and I just needed that roof
fixed.*

Nothing is fixed. Every day
is different I guess, quiet baby,
loud baby, you can't pin down
a single trait to claim the
whole self. *What about when
you were pregnant? Did I kick a
lot? Did Dad sing
to me in the womb?*
My mother drifts
into what she calls *incidents*,
incidents, what Wordsworth
called *among the lowest allurements in poetry*,
my mother called times
my father got drunk,
volatile and prone to
fuming and furies where
anything might slip—
tongue, temper, tile.

.

My mother sits on the step looking out
at her garden. She is named

for a herb and likes to talk and talk
about everything and nothing—

from which poets read *The Golden
Bough* to that man in Covent Garden

who collects golliwogs. Everything
is a piece of some larger and endless

subject. My mother volunteers
in charity shops and delivers

food to people who live alone.
My mother lives alone

and won't talk about herself.
She points at one flower

in a pot, says *That's from
Gran's garden. I took the seeds*

*after she died. She'd taken them
from her gran's garden.*

I had lived in her house
most of my life and she'd never

told me that. She says it quietly
and quickly changes

the subject as if to tuck this small
detail away, between politics

and neighbourhood gossip,
as if trying to bury it

amongst the life of
everything else.

.

This morning your mother and I lay in bed waiting
for a call from the plumber because the kitchen walls
were damp and peeling (like in the film *Repulsion*).
Hallways of wailing walls tear a woman open,
which is the worse metaphor to sleep next to,
so we do something soft, we begin calling out
random names, pretending to answer the phone
that hadn't yet rung: *Hello? Yes, hang on a second,*
Solomon! Claude! Ezra! searching the sounds
that might summon you, we listen for the echo
of what the tired rooms might have to bear.

.

At first I can't hear your heart,
I ask for the monitor to be brought closer.
The monitor looks like the retro radio
my father slept next to when I was a child.

I put my hand on the speaker, feel the pulse
between the father that was half asleep
and the music he leaned into.

.

Isaac, Isaiah, your great-grandfather was a preacher.
There is a poem on the back of his sermon
in cursive so hard to decipher,
images jotted down perhaps rushed

between his other tasks—
four children and a congregation—
though the urge, the ideas, kept coming
like half-seen visions. I almost hear him whisper

the lines to himself while his sons kick
a ball against the side of the house. *Thud thud*
against his clarity and concentration, the walls
hold an imagined silence that keeps him praying.

Ira (gender-neutral; pronounced EYE-rah): meaning 'watchful' in Hebrew. In Sanskrit, it's both 'wind' (male meaning) and 'the Earth' (female meaning).

Birch (gender-neutral; pronounced berch): meaning, in Old English, 'bright, shining; the birch tree'.

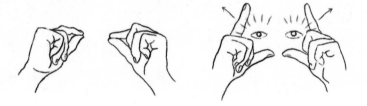

ii

The New Father

The new father

didn't want to be called *father*
so he raised the bridge to protect the borders

of fatherhood. He shouted over the water.
The harshness of his voice was hereditary.

Why is he a monument when he could be
a yoga stretch, an open hand, a name

over another name?
There can be no dispensation

for the father. He's gone through life pretending
it was the house shivering and not his father.

His father never said he wanted
to be his father and here he is, wanting

to be his father. He wants to be warm
as midnight cups and running

car engines and the man
in Freetown who rowed him across the river

and asked him to name the countries
he'd been to, before he told him

he'd never been anywhere
but motherland, fatherland. Amen.

•

I hold my son in a fluorescent corridor, a floaty
fatherland, a new field of focus.

.

> *Fatherland!* he said,
> when he meant a lake
> of delirium.

.

I burp and feed you and bounce and read and sing and nothing
gives you rest your cries tear air I hold you up

    my mind a swung bell

            •

Pay attention to baby

your mother's voice knocks
me out of the trance I haven't realised

I've drifted into
so stoic and frozen

until it is witnessed

            •

        Her back
        to me

        you
        a tiny breeze

        in your cot

            •

The wind picks up

leaves blow around me

a branch snaps

leaving a mouth

roaring

in the bark

·

I became fatherless at 26 and a father
at 35 and whenever I look out

the living room window I feel myself
become the child left alone in the house

·

O boy

                alone on the train across
        the tracks sticking up your finger

        at the window as I play peekaboo
        with my months-old baby. Once

        I too paraded that thought of fuck
                family fuck growing up fuck

                what I might become, fuck
        vanishing into shapes I'll never

see myself in. Boy, fuck you / praise you
        alone on the train across the tracks

                •

In the thin dream is a tilted canvas glittering
in the Serpentine gallery / hung as a prism of green, dangling weeds
I point at the circles / the floating faces like bead curtains
over a doorway / expect an Oracle on the other side stirring tea
in her kitchen ready to instruct or deconstruct me while
she sits at the table of piled junk mail and bills / She reads a letter
from the sea and I enter it / The water is pockets of cold then
warm then cold then Caribbean Sea then Thames

then I'm Speedo-ed skintight in Haggerston Pool / backstroke
so I see the flaking ceiling and smell the chlorine / I pass
the strings of blue flags so I know I'm approaching the wall
and I'm counting each arm that enters water and
I tumble turn and push away in the heated, silky lane
and breathe into the shape of a tree / I'm fully feather
headed and careful and waaaaah green light turns red
with crying through the baby monitor

                                              the baby's bed
is in the corner of the room beside the window in the dark
shhh shhh I tell baby reaching up his arms a story
that is my story and baby will grow into it / How tall
is the story now? Is it marked on the wall? I'll have
to ask the landlord / I'll have to ask the Oracle / I'll have to ask
the voice, where am I speaking now? Inward? / Sprouting

language / All plants and weeds have eyes / I'm staring
into their murky, stuck mud heads / What is depth now I skim
everything / I'm a lightly touched painting of a thorn tree
in a wild, wild wind / Now the rubber
handle on the pram is flaking because it sleeps too close
to the radiator / I push my son through January

and Kensington Park past the Serpentine over
the bridge and the dogs are howling at the horses / I notice
the shiny leather saddles on the horses and the knitted
jumpers on the dogs / They cost more than anything
my son or I wear / Even the leash is a kind of costly
tethering / The lake is bright with gliding swans / now I see
the couple with two kids and two dogs I think in receipts
and bin bags to put outside and shit to scrape /

I deny the couple a light story / a radiant marriage
/ there's resentment and there's blossoming
in a field of frost / where is the speaking now?
Back in that thin dream and bully wind
pulling up trees like hair from the roots

•

First words as a father
are, of course, prayers.

•

Give us strength
    to do nothing
but watch
    the baby
discover
    his right hand,
stare at the
    nounness of it—
as bright
    a moment as the child
I saw this morning,
    kicking pavement leaves,
his feet uncovered a glowing
    gold stud, glistening
on autumn concrete.
    The child opened
his whole hand
    and bent down
to grasp it.
    This is a different
economy.
    My own child
biting down
    on his new
fingers
    on his new hand,
perhaps like a pirate
    bites a gold coin
to see
    if it's real.

·

The baby is fine

doing nothing. *Do*

nothing. Smash capitalism.

Do nothing but look at your heart

and say what you see there

said
some saint.

•

The quietest thing—
cash in my dead father's wallet.

Nothing breaks the notes.

·

The noise

died so I looked online
and couldn't believe the price

for a new noise, so I bought
a secondhand noise, deliverable

and *like new*. It arrived
on my windowsill

the next day in a box wrapped
with too much tape. I tore

each layer of the sticky plastic
like unwrapping a bandage.

The noise was delicate
as a small glass

of steam and ash.
The thing I liked most about

the secondhand noise
was how much it deepened

the sensation of walking
through the house

with a newfound
breeze. I didn't know

how loud my noise was.
I was breathing

like snoring
while awake.

When my neighbours
complained something heavy

was moving on the other side
of their wall, slamming doors

and knocking tables, I got out
my noise, astounded again

by its hovering lightness
and said nothing.

.

Son, you have your fist
in your mouth,

you take it out, your fists
like two radiant rocks,

your eyes lost
between stars

and the points
I,   your father
try   to constellate.

•

Lyra	harp
Libra	scales
Ember	spark
Fornax	the furnace
Myer	bringer of light

•

When I finally meet my neighbour in the lift
she has two small children and is sympathetic

with her nodding, knowing the early energy
of parenthood. She has high brown eyebrows, short,

East Asian stature, speaks with an Oxford English
accent and when I speak in my somewhere-in-London

voice she leans in, *Ah, oh yes*, as the doors
close and we descend gently towards the ground.

We look like the rare brown figures
on a private property poster as the doors open

on Bloomsbury and we walk our children out
into the courtyard. She lights a cigarette

and exhales
as a man with a tattered sleeping bag

around his neck like a scarf scurries
out of the bushes. My neighbour gasps,

holds her children back and shudders.
See, this is why you got to move places

where people are rich or on their way
to wealth . . . And because there is no turbulence,

no wobble in her voice, I find myself
preferring the trees above us, the way the wind

moves through them and the leaves hold on
so tenderly.

·

I broke up with righteousness. It sparkled on stage
but annoyed everyone at the table. I broke up
with the city, even the garden with murals and birds
in stone fountains. I broke up with correcting cab drivers
calling me Greek. I broke up with myths
and defensiveness, decided to be an empty picture frame
no one has to straighten. I broke up with childlessness
broke up with blame and broke up with desire
to have no desire. I broke up with the word
Pleasure and got back with the word Palaver.
I broke up and angels sang louder. I broke up
with announcing my convictions and good news
on the internet I broke up with talking to myself
as if I'm not there I broke up with people-pleasing
and the trembling boundary between life and still life.
I broke up with the scrolling, scrolling and the what
am I looking for? What has already gone? I got back
with my head and found the air inside it lost in the field.
I broke broke broke my concentration with distance.
I broke with timelines. I broke and heard the air say
Good parents are a blessing and the weather is getting bluer.

·

The night I gave up trying
to get the baby to sleep
after constant wailing

I lost it said
the baby needs
his mother

and handed him over
I made excuses
for my fatherly failure:

drowsy sleep
lousy hunger, hidden
trigger

here, you arrive, clouds
about to burst on a street
of unroofed houses

you weigh less
than broken satellite signals
than a single seed

But rows could rip a marriage
certificate

                              scream across the room

or down the stairs
like my father
who called you the last

resort of exhaustion.
Lower your sting
lay down quick

the venom
that marks me
ugly and unlikeable.

Thank you
for eventually
leaving us

my wife and me
with the test
of returning

•

In the grey birches,
a nest.

•

There have already been days
I thought about leaving
thinking I need
myself back need
to stop the trigger
of seeing my child
get what I needed

.

And God said unto Noah, The end of all flesh is come before me . . .
                                        —Genesis 6:13

I think twice
before bathing
with my son,
think to search
if it's appropriate,
then worry about
the digital trace of
the question.
I cover myself,
not wanting to reveal
what I contend with.
My son has no data
on desire, or rather
my son is still gathering
data on his shape.

I've gathered
much on mine.
Something ageless in me
is coded like scripture,
and knows that
Noah's nakedness
stained his son.
I lie with mine
in warm, soapy water.
He stands, wobbles
on my chest. I am
his surfboard
during the Flood,
an unsettled shore,
an ark of clean
and unclean
animals, *the end
of all flesh.*
Strange. I uncross
my legs. Laugh. Pray
my son doesn't pee.
But even if he does,
we couldn't be cleaner.

•

It's a strange word, desire

is what I thought I heard my swimming instructor
say from the poolside— strange *world* perhaps?

I wonder, as I freestyle another lap, face
in the blue, blue and blue tiles, blue and yellow

electric eyes glowing on underwater walls.
A deepening groove—I'm blue

and co-ordinated blue and breathy
as whatever world on land, filled

and inflated feels like
nonsense, now, before turning

my back into water counting strokes,
breaths, lengths until I liquefy

into scrutiny, I mean synchronicity,
synced connectivity, interdisciplinary,

am I hearing myself? What striving slides
along the lane, what am I

in this chlorinised state? My head
a scratched chalkboard wiped

smooth, an unsinkable raft, what
signals me now? What lines

are unthinkable in this undrinkable
unresolvable surge of want

and want.

·

I took the honour

                    and thought
                    to melt

                    it down,
                    to lava it

                    but there wasn't
                    enough silver

                    sparkling
                    on the medal

                    to mould
                    an impossibly

                    brilliant plaque
                    for my father's

                    grave.

Before the acceptance, my father
spoke in a dream, said *Say yes*

but don't take it so serious.
He laughed like a fire

full of pips at the thought
of his son's royal remaking.

Dad, I still fret
this thing

and the scalds
of quotations

about what
Empire is now

after all
it has burned.

·

Queen Elizabeth and I are enchanted
with each other. I have been

looking at her since I was a boy
at Christmas sitting in my

grandmother's living room, facing
the fire.

Your grandmother starts to talk
and what could be

elegiac easily
becomes a rant

for the century
my family has been born in.

.

In the cemetery, a woman pushes a man
in a wheelchair and stops

by the path so he can take it all in.
A woman

with a pink duvet draping her whole body
grumbles on the grass, rocks back and forth

as a younger woman in leggings lets go
of her son's hand and watches him stumble

towards the graves

.

Let me look at
what you're seeing
                    all by yourself

                         •

My divorced friend

lights my screen
with darkness . . . *stuck*

*on why I deserve
anything but sadness.*

Friend, I'm sorry.
Your business now

is breath, not air,
your business

is finding out
what lifts

your chest.
It should be simple

but it never is.
Me, I'm all sink

and soap-suds, nappy cream
and night feeds.

All change
is tender.

.

I see you turn to the beeping
monitor, your mother whispering,

the glowing phone
alert. Your eyes swallow the sound

that my ears can't. Sometimes I'm afraid
that you won't have the patience

to connect with your deaf father.
Will we become two people

in the same house, only
one of us sensing alarm?

.

The Home Secretary's
child and

my child listen
to the same story

read by
the librarian

about a dog
who wanted

to be good,
but wasn't.

The dog dug soil
from pots

of houseplants,
chased a cat

and ate an
entire cake.

my ~~black~~ child plays
with the ~~brown~~ child

of a politician
who is closing

the country to
~~black and brown~~

children. I could smile,
I could spit

in her face, ~~our face~~
which is this country.

Our two toddlers,
without speech, stare

into each other
like the boundless

O in ~~open~~
~~holy~~
~~crossing~~

torn.

•

The first word of the girl
we never had comes

to me at night like a creak,
like the opening noise

of an ancient dictionary
with page after page

of words for girl—yam,
lavender, magnolia, mist.

.

The radiant daffodils
remind me of Jamaica

Kincaid saying she raised
those plants to make peace

with Wordsworth

.

The world is too much with us; late and soon

•

The man vomiting in the park has only
the tree to lean on. His green sick gushing out
like water from a busted hydrant. The woman
working out by the bench, mid-lunge,
turns away, the man grunting through pull-ups
on the climbing frame closes his eyes. The crack
and spit of sickness is everywhere, everyone

is caught up in the mess. No one moves towards
naming. Look at me preaching, writing
noticing is a small and quiet way to begin
moving away from the passive crowd. O God,
look, my gym bag that reads *Lift. Laugh.*
Live. What form will I take now?
Is some fit and moral saint about to appear?

•

The waiter said something about prawns
and I ordered them. The kitchen between us

hinged on what was heard. Across the table
Hannah's brow wrinkled, she affirmed

that the waiter had said *he's deathly
allergic to prawns.*

I covered my mouth.

The waiter returned, holding his breath
away from the steam, rising like a vowelling ghost.

Waiter! I apologise for my holed air,
my strange mouth, my mist, here.

•

When I'm the poet at the table with the banker
and the successful novelist, there's no good way

to admit my envies, to say it's hard
to be close to someone who has what I want—the money

for constant childcare, the advance big enough to stand still
for as long as it takes to get the words out. Tonight

what matters most is keeping the conversation going so
we pass the guacamole and the jalapeños, stuffed

with peanut butter, which I am the first
to bite, not quite believing this recipe exists in a restaurant

this fancy, something so improvised, like whoever came up
with it was high. But the surprise is how the thick texture

of the peanut butter shuts down the spice before it flares
on my tongue, and I nod to both, the banker and the successful novelist,

that I can handle it.

•

I pass the bins stuffed with Star-
bucks and Burger King cups

and come to the fountain
of other people's children

laughing as they charge through
the whoop of water I turn

my son in his pram to face the scene
we sit beside a woman twirling

her hair like jewelry
we hear green parakeets flutter from

the tree overhead see pigeons
peck at the polished shoes

of the man in his blue business suit
a man in an apron sleeps

with his arms folded
snoring the bench vibrates

a seagull lands
beside him beak-yellow scissors

the air is sharp
the sight has opened

my ears it's a whole
madness, my old

screaming selves.

.

Our first time leaving our baby
with the sitter and the show is momentous,

except for this one stalling singer
with her shrilling voice. Every time

she unleashes during scene changes
it unnerves us, has us checking our phones.

We can't sit still in this note any more
than we could understand what parenthood was

before landing in it.

.

You are beginning to squirm
and cry while I think

about my favourite London street
the narrowness of it its straightness

like peering down the throat of a
quieter city symmetrical houses

attached together the thin panes
seem wise and vulnerable

above the double yellow lines
cautions that brighten both sides

of the road.

•

I took you to a baby screening of *The Worst Person in the World*. The dying comic book artist says to the love of his life *I don't want to be a voice in your head. I don't want to live on through my art.... I want to live in my flat with you.*

The dialogue
echoes and shudders.

.

You're in bed, falling asleep.
I receive an alert, news

about magpies. Nationwide, spikes
were installed to stop nesting on ledges,

but now they are using their beaks
to rip them out then build a kind

of metallic militant nest. Should I
wake you to share the story?

Today you pointed at each magpie
in the park with such wonder

and I could tell you this might be
the best image we have for what

our nation is and what it takes
to make it home.

.

The prisoner who flinches
each time the gate clangs
is reading a poem for his wife
who doesn't like poetry.

He is ready to fight
for his slim lines
on time and inside weight,
the shutting of English.

I look at him the way I looked
at a man on the outside
holding a lamp, setting out
across a bridge.

.

What do you want? asks the therapist
as I stare out the window at two birds
bobbing on the roof across the street. Sun on warm
tiles, birds' claws tucked away, drainpipes prepared
to handle rain: that's what I want. A conversation
in a coffee shop, umbrellas open over the tables,
the trees twisted and tangled, their shadows spilling.
I want to take off my sunglasses to look better
at the man pushing his table into the sun
on Bloomsbury Square. Two women come along
and he instantly offers his seat. They aren't
surprised, they know his name. That's what I want.
To stand outside without a mask and nod
at a man I won't have to fight
for a seat in the sun.

.

The birds sound different in this city.
I'm new to their rhythms, can't place them easily.
Jarring, precise, I have to listen.

I've never been one for birds, nor envisioned
ever thinking birds were godly,
but the birds sound different in this city.

I bought audiobooks about birds—didn't listen.
Their names and looks uncharted astronomy.
Jarring, precise, I have to listen.

The birds have invented a new religion.
They sing from trees in sleet storms, devoutly.
The birds sound different in this city.

Settling here was not my mission.
But wherever I live I live honestly.
Jarring, precise, I have to listen.

walking these streets I feel forgiven.
The bells of the birds are auguries.
They tell me I've finally found a way of living.
Jarring, precise, I have to listen.

•

My child has yet to form
words out loud despite

the meaning-making of
placing two palms up

and shaking them to ask
where? Where language

meets my deafness where
I'm sure my child

is a concrete path
to the fountain.

.

Because I didn't know much about gardening
when we first rented the house,

I called a gardener who drove miles to tend
our plot, to dig a path and tame

the green that swayed as if to celebrate
what wind brushed through it. I realise

the gardener can't refuse the work.
Blades will always present themselves

in these transactions. Kindness
doesn't come into it really, but when my partner

and I open the blinds, smiling as we prepare
breakfast for ourselves and the toddler

whose feet bumble the ground
around the bed towards the mirror, to see

the dance of what can be done with
muscles in the legs and arms and face,

it seems the earth is not here for us
but with us. And how would we get from

one place to another without the kindness
of paths, of seeding and mowing?

.

The first word my son signed
was *music*: both hands, fingers conducting
music for everything—even hunger open
mouth for the choo-chew spoon
squealing *mmm*—*music*, we'd play
a record while he ate *music* when
he wanted milk so I pour and hum
a lullaby or 'I Don't Know'
by Bill Withers because it's okay
not to know what you want
and I want him to know that. *Music*
is wiping the table after the plates *music*
is feel my forehead for fever is whatever
occurs in the centre of the body, whatever
makes arms raise up, up.
The second word my son signed
was *bird*—beaked finger to thumb, bird
for everything outside—window, sky, tree,
roof, chimney, aerial, airplane—birds. I
saw I had given him a sign name. Fingers
to eyes raising from thumbs—wide
eye meaning watchful of the earth
in the combination of two different roots—Hebrew, Sanskrit.
I love how he clings
to my shoulders and turns
his head to point at the soft body
of a caterpillar sliding across the counter,
and *signs*, music.

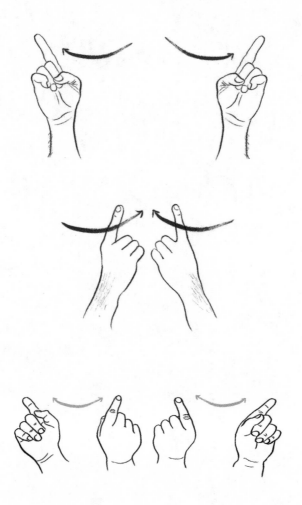

Notes

'Towards Naming' was written over the last six months of my co-parent's pregnancy. 'The New Father' was written during the first year of our son's life.

'I have never separated the writing of poetry from prayer' is a quote that served as a touchstone for this book as a whole. It comes from Derek Walcott's 'The Art of Poetry No. 37' interview by Edward Hirsch (*The Paris Review* no. 101, winter 1986).

p. 1: 'Look at that tree and write about it' is for Mimi Khalvati.

p. 6: The phrase 'red-hot money' is from Rosemary Tonks, as quoted in 'Re-Covered: *The Bloater* by Rosemary Tonks' by Lucy Scholes (*The Paris Review* online, 23 May 2022).

p. 10: 'Don't worry about a thing' is quoted from the song 'Three Little Birds' by Bob Marley & The Wailers, from the 1977 album *Exodus*.

p. 10: The video referred to here is for the song 'Is This Love' by Bob Marley & The Wailers, from the 1978 album *Kaya*.

p. 10: ' . . . once stole a guitar from a man who / refused to pay him for his song' refers to an incident recounted in the 'Eat the Fish but Spit Out the Bones' chapter of Colin Grant's *The Natural Mystics: Marley, Tosh, and Wailer* (W. W. Norton & Company, 2011).

p. 11: 'In my hand I have nothing, in the bush is everything' is quoted from *Letter to the Father / Brief an den Vater: Bilingual Edition* by Franz Kafka, translated from the German by Ernst Kaiser and Eithne Wilkins (Schocken Books, 2015).

p. 15: 'It matters what you call a thing' is quoted from the title poem in Solmaz Sharif's *Look* (Graywolf Press, 2016).

p. 17: 'Freedom is measured, in part, by the freedom to choose one's own name' is quoted from Camille T. Dungy's *Guidebook to Relative Strangers: Journeys into Race, Motherhood, and History* (W. W. Norton & Company, 2017).

pp. 18 and 41: The form of the 'Nasya' and 'Lyra' sections (with names and their corresponding meanings) was inspired by the opening of the section titled 'Head-Turner' in *To the Realization of Perfect Helplessness* by Robin Coste Lewis (Knopf, 2022).

p. 18: The meanings for the names given here come from TheBump.com and Wikipedia, some directly and some more loosely inspired.

p. 21: William Wordsworth's referral to incidents as 'among the lowest allurements in poetry' is cited in *William Wordsworth: A Literary Life* by John Williams (Macmillan Press Ltd, 1996).

p. 26: The origins and quoted meanings for the names given here come from TheBump.com and Wikipedia.

pp. 34–5: 'In the thin dream' was inspired by the painting 'Blues for the Martyrs' by Kamala Ibrahim Ishag, included in her exhibition 'States of Oneness' at the Serpentine South Gallery in London from 7 October 2022–29 January 2023, and *The Waves* by Virginia Woolf (Hogarth Press, 1931).

p. 37: The italicized lines (beginning with 'Do / nothing. Smash capital-ism. . . .') through the closing lines ('said / some saint.') are a riff on lines from Jim Moore's poem 'Admit It' in *Prognosis* (Graywolf Press, 2021).

p. 41: The meanings for the names given here come from TheBump.com, Wikipedia, and Dictionary.com.

pp. 46–7: The lines from Genesis 6:13 are from the King James Version of the Bible.

p. 54: The children's story referenced here is the book *Oh No, George!* written and illustrated by Chris Haughton (Walker Books, 2013).

p. 56: The Jamaica Kincaid quote referenced is from an interview with *Fifteen Minutes*, the magazine of *The Harvard Crimson*, by Hayoung E. Ahn (14 September 2017). In the interview, Kincaid says: 'My garden has at least 10,000 daffodils because I wanted to redeem Wordsworth. It's a story about being forced to memorize his poem, "I Wandered Lonely as a Cloud." So I decided that to pay homage to Wordsworth, I would plant at least 10,000 daffodils. That's just on the lawn. . . . Sometimes, I have friends come over and we have a daffodil party, and we recite Wordsworth and drink champagne. It's not Wordsworth's fault that colonial education forced us to memorize a poem about a flower that we had never seen.'

p. 57: 'The world is too much with us; late and soon' is quoted from Wil-liam Wordsworth's *The Poetical Works of William Wordsworth, Vol. IV (of VIII)*, edited by William Knight (Macmillan and Co., Ltd., 1896).

p. 63: 'I don't want to be a voice in your head. I don't want to live on through my art. . . . I want to live in my flat with you.' is quoted from *The Worst Person in the World*, dir. Joachim Trier (2021). The lines quoted here are English subtitles, translated from the original Norwegian, from the film as shown on Hulu (in the closing credits, English subtitles and dialogue lists are credited to Erik Grønvold).

p. 65: '*What do you want?* asks the therapist' was commissioned, in earlier form, for BBC Radio 4's programme *The Anatomy of Kindness* (see the 'Results' episode, 9 March 2022).

p. 66: 'The birds sound different in this city' was first commissioned as 'Resonance' by the University of Warwick and this earlier form is placed on the wall as a 'Mural Poem' inside the University of Warwick Faculty of Arts building.

pp. 67–8: 'Because I didn't know much about gardening' references Philip Larkin's 'The Mower' from Larkin's *Collected Poems* (Farrar, Straus and Giroux, 2004) and Andrew Marvell's 'The Mower's Song'. Ross Gay's essay 'We Kin (The Garden: The Third Incitement)' from *Inciting Joy* (Algonquin Books, 2022) is alluded to, particularly the line 'when we refuse to celebrate the earth's kindness, we prepare the ground for the earth to refuse kindness to us'.

p. 69: 'wide / eye meaning watchful of the earth / in the combination of two different roots—Hebrew, Sanskrit' refers to various meanings for 'Ira' given on Wikipedia, as well as the Egyptian Eye of Ra (see more here, too, on the 'Eye of Ra' Wikipedia page).

Acknowledgements

I give thanks to the editors of the following publications in which selections from this book first appeared, often in other versions: *The New Yorker, London Review of Books, Granta, Guernica, Ploughshares, Prairie Schooner, Magma, Writers Rebel, Poetry Northwest, The New Statesman, The Nation, The Rialto, Social Works II* (Gagosian Gallery), *Poetry London, The London Magazine, The Poetry Review, The Times Literary Supplement, The Slowdown, Southern Indiana Review.*

'Matrescence' and 'Patrescence' are real, so I've got to give thanks to my partner in parenthood, Tabitha Austin. Your (visible and invisible) sacrifices for our family, your wisdom, protection, presence, talents and intelligence—none of this work exists without you.

Shout-out to the early readers of sections of the book: Shira Erlichman, Sa Whitley, Chris Rose, Saleem Hue Penny, Jasmine Reid, Gustavo Adolfo Aybar, W. J. Lofton, Nome Emeka Patrick, Fanny Brewster, D. Colin, Geoff Anderson, Victoria Chang, Marwa Helal.

Shout-out to my 'Green Doors': Will Harris, Gboyega Odubanjo, Thea Stanton, Keith Jarrett, Victoria Adukwei Bulley, Pádraig Ó Tuama, Guy Gunaratne, Joe Dunthorne, Zaffar Kunial, Caleb Azumah Nelson—each of your eyes and ears offered invaluable encouragement and guidance.

Shout-out to Caroline Parker MBE for gifting me my sign name and Polly Dunbar for her beautiful BSL illustrations; to my agent, Niki Chang; my editors, Colette Bryce and Elizabeth DeMeo; and the Picador and Tin House teams for championing this work and believing.

Shout-out to my mentors: Mimi Khalvati, Hannah Lowe, Colin Grant, Peter Kahn, Malika Booker, Karen McCarthy Woolf, Nick Makoha, Roger Robinson, Jason Allen-Paisant, Denise Saul, and Elontra Hall.

Shout-out to my communities: Cave Canem, Zoeglossia, Obsidian, XR Writers Rebel, Writers Mosaic, and my friends and family—you know who you are.

Shout-out to everyone surviving, raising humans, making (and absorbing) art despite the pandemic, the cost-of-living-crisis, the climate emergency, and all the fuckery of isms and schisms.

Shout-out to you, reader. Thank YOU.

Finally, for the fathers healing their hurts, keep going.

Raymond Antrobus was born in Hackney, London, to an English mother and Jamaican father. He is the author of *To Sweeten Bitter*, *The Perseverance*, and *All The Names Given*. He was awarded the 2017 Geoffrey Dearmer Prize (judged by Ocean Vuong) for his poem 'Sound Machine'. In 2019 he became the first poet to be awarded the Rathbones Folio Prize for best work of literature in any genre. Other accolades include the Ted Hughes Award, the Lucille Clifton Legacy Award, and a Sunday Times/University of Warwick Young Writer of the Year Award. *All The Names Given* was shortlisted for the Costa Book Award for Poetry and the T. S. Eliot Prize, and several of his poems were added to the GCSE syllabus in 2022. His picture books for children are published by Walker Books (UK) and Candlewick Press (US). Antrobus is an advocate for several D/deaf charities, including DeafKidz International and the National Deaf Children's Society. He divides his time between England and New Orleans.